Commercial Goat Raising for Beginners

How to Raise Goats for Profits as a Beginner

By

Merle Richards

Copyright © 2023 Merle Richards

or omissions. Changes are periodically made to this book.

Upon using the information in this book, you agree to hold the author harmless from and against any damages, costs, and expenses, including any potential legal fees resulting from applying any of the information provided by this guide.

This disclaimer applies to any damage or injury caused by the use and application, whether directly or indirectly, of any advice or information presented, whether for breach of contract, tort, negligence, personal injury, criminal intent, or under any other cause of action.

Published with support from:

RegulaReaders Publishing

regulareaders.com

info@regulareaders.com

Click the logo to join and engage with our idie authors and amazing community of fellow regular readers and gain access to ARCs, book summaries, and an informative weekly blog.

REGULAREADERS

AN OASIS FOR REGULAR READERS

You can also join our community by going to

https://regulareaders.com/comunity/

Introduction

Are you an enterprising agripreneur looking to start a commercial goat-raising venture, but you're unsure about where or how to start?

If you are, let me be the bearer of good news□:

Commercial goat raising is fulfilling and profitable, which makes it an excellent agribusiness idea you can implement and use to build a sustainable business while working with intelligent and versatile animals.

If you're looking for a guidebook that will demystify commercial goat raising and help you understand what it takes to start and run a commercially successful goat-raising venture, look no further.

"Commercial Goat Raising for Beginners" is a comprehensive guide designed to equip aspiring goat farmers with the knowledge and tools to start and successfully manage a profitable goat-raising operation.

Whether your focus is on meat production, fiber harvesting, or dairy products, each section of this book has something that will answer all your commercial goat-raising questions.

While many resources focus solely on the practical aspects of goat farming, this book takes a unique approach to goat farming by leaning into the business side of the venture.

I understand that for beginners, it is not enough to know how to care for goats; you must also grasp the financial and strategic aspects that underpin a profitable enterprise.

By merging practical husbandry techniques with sound business practices, this guidebook aims to empower you to make informed decisions and succeed in a competitive market.

Whether you are an established farmer looking to diversify your portfolio, an individual with no farming experience but a burning desire to raise goats for profits, or an agripreneur, "Commercial Goat Raising for Beginners" is your roadmap to success.

Among other things:

- ✓ We shall explore the exciting world of running a commercially-viable goat-rasing farm.

- ✓ We will discuss the key elements of commercial goat raising, covering a wide range of topics to ensure you have a holistic understanding of this industry.

- ✓ We will delve into breed selection, infrastructure requirements, nutrition and healthcare, breeding strategies, and more.

✓ Additionally, we will explore the diverse market opportunities available, including goat meat, wool, milk, and value-added products, enabling you to make informed choices that align with your commercial goat-raising goals and target market.

This book aims to inspire, inform, and ensure you know which steps to take to build a successful commercial goat-raising operation.

Table of Contents

Section 2

How to Raise Goats For Commercial Milk Production

Chapter 6: Introduction to Commercial Goat Milk Production

Popular Goat Breeds For Milk Production and Their Characteristics

Factors to Consider When Selecting Goat Breeds for Profitable Milk Production

Chapter 6: Housing and Infrastructure for Milk Production

Shelter and Barns

Milking Parlor Setup

Waste Management

Chapter 7: Feeding and Nutrition Requirements for Dairy Goats

Considerations for Feeding and Nutrition Requirements

Chapter 8: Milk Processing and Value Addition

Chapter 1: Is Commercial Goat Raising Even Profitable?

This chapter will explore the potential of commercial goat farming.

From the increasing demand for goat products to the various avenues for profitability, you will discover why goats have become a sought-after livestock, making them a great business option for aspiring agripreneurs and farmers.

Goat Products Consumption Patterns and Market Demand

Goat products, including meat, milk, and fiber, are increasingly becoming popular worldwide, thanks mostly to cultural, culinary, and health-related factors.

Goat meat, commonly known as chevon or caprine meat, is a staple in many cuisines and cultures. It is prized for its distinct flavor, tenderness, and nutritional benefits, making it a popular choice for individuals seeking lean protein sources.

In addition to meat, goat milk and dairy products have gained recognition for their unique composition and potential health benefits. Those with lactose intolerances or allergies often prefer goat milk because it is easier to digest and contains lower levels of lactose. The versatility of goat milk extends to various dairy products, such as butter, yogurt, and cheese, which offer a creamy texture and rich flavor profile.

Furthermore, the demand for goat fiber, such as mohair and cashmere, continues to thrive in the textile industry. These luxurious fibers are prized for their softness, warmth, and durability, making them highly sought after by designers of specialty garments and artisanal products.

Factors contributing to the rising market demand for goat meat and products include increased consumer awareness of the health benefits of goat products, cultural preferences for goat meat and milk in certain regions, and the growing trend of sustainable and locally sourced products.

As a prospecting commercial goat farmer, understanding and capitalizing on market demand allows you to practice targeted production and value-addition to create a sustainably profitable business in this industry.

Why Choose Goat Raising as a Business Venture

Commercial goat raising offers several advantages, making it an appealing business venture for beginners.

Let's explore some key reasons why your decision to embark on this entrepreneurial journey is a good one:

- **Low initial investment**: Unlike other livestock enterprises, goat farming requires relatively lower capital investment. For example, you can raise goats on smaller parcels of land, which reduces the upfront costs associated with purchasing or leasing large tracts of land.

- **Adaptability and efficiency**: Goats are highly adaptable animals that thrive in diverse climatic conditions and terrains. They can eat almost anything, including shrubs, weeds, and grasses. This adaptability reduces feed costs and makes it easier to employ sustainable farming practices. Additionally, goats have efficient feed conversion rates— they effectively convert feed into meat, milk, or fiber—for maximum productivity.

- **Potential profitability**: Commercial goat raising has a lot of profitability potential. For example, goats have a relatively short gestation period that enables them to produce multiple offspring in a single breeding cycle. This rapid reproductive rate translates into quicker turnover and potential returns on investment. Furthermore, goats have a strong market demand because their meat, milk, and fiber have unique characteristics. By targeting specific markets and producing high-quality products, goat farmers can achieve profitability in the industry.

- **Scalability and flexibility**: Goat farming is scalable and flexible, and you can start the business with a manageable number of goats and gradually expand your herds as you gain experience and resources. This flexibility makes it easier to adapt your commercial operations to changing market conditions, customer demands, and personal goals. Whether it's a small-scale family farm or a larger commercial operation, goat farming allows for growth at one's own pace.

- **Niche markets and value-added products**: The goat industry is broad and robust enough that you can tap into niche markets and create value-added products. Specialty cheeses, gourmet meat cuts, organic milk, artisanal soaps, and luxurious fiber products are value-added offerings that can command higher prices and cater to specific consumer preferences. By identifying unique market niches and developing innovative products, you can differentiate your enterprise in the industry and potentially achieve higher profit margins.

Challenges and Considerations Associated with Commercial Goat Raising

Even though commercial goat farming is highly profitable and diverse, it is important to know its challenges and things you should consider before diving into it. Understanding and proactively addressing these challenges will help you build a resilient and successful commercial goat farming operation.

Here are some key challenges and considerations to keep in mind:

Disease Management

Goats are susceptible to various diseases and health issues, including parasites, respiratory infections, and metabolic disorders.

Therefore, you **MUST** develop a comprehensive health management plan that includes regular vaccinations, deworming protocols, and proper nutrition. Having a robust health plan for your goats ensures their well-being, which also ensures the success of your operation.

Breeding Difficulties

Successful goat breeding can be a complex process.

Factors such as selecting suitable breeding stock, managing reproductive cycles, and ensuring successful mating and kidding require careful attention.

Understanding breeding techniques, including natural mating and artificial insemination, can significantly impact your operational productivity and genetic quality.

Market Fluctuations

Like any agricultural enterprise, the market for goat products can experience demand and pricing fluctuations.

Being adaptable and closely monitoring market trends will allow you to make informed decisions and adjust your production and marketing strategies accordingly.

Diversifying your product range and establishing strong relationships with buyers can help mitigate the risks associated with market fluctuations.

Infrastructure and Facilities

You cannot run a successful goat-raising enterprise without proper infrastructure and facilities because these ensure the well-being of your goats and the efficient management of your farm.

Some key infrastructure you will need are suitable housing, fencing, feeding, watering systems, and waste management facilities. Investing in well-designed and functional infrastructure will contribute to the health and productivity of your goats and streamline your daily operations.

Financial Management

Managing the financial aspects of your goat-raising business is not something you should neglect if you want long-term success.

Financial management can take many forms, but it usually involves budgeting for operational costs, tracking expenses, pricing your products appropriately, and monitoring profitability. Understanding the financial aspects of your operation will help you make informed decisions.

Knowledge and Skill Development

Goat farming is an endeavor that requires continuous learning and skill development.

Staying updated on industry practices, advancements in animal husbandry, and new technologies will help enhance the productivity and efficiency of your operation. Networking with other goat farmers, attending workshops, and accessing educational resources can all contribute to your ongoing growth.

Acknowledging and addressing these challenges and considerations will help you prepare to overcome obstacles and build a resilient and profitable goat-raising business operation.

Understanding Different Commercial Purposes

The world of goat raising has several exciting commercial opportunities to consider.

The next section will explore the specific requirements and techniques for each purpose, including meat production, milk production, fiber production, and breeding. Understanding these avenues lets you decide which commercial purpose(s) align with your goals and resources.

Let's delve into the diverse opportunities that await you as a commercial goat farmer.

Section 1

The Ins and Outs of Raising Goats For Commercial Meat Production

Chapter 2: Introduction to Commercial Goat Meat Production

There's a notable increase in the demand for goat meat globally. We can attribute this surge in popularity to various factors, including cultural preferences, dietary considerations, and the recognition of its nutritional value.

If you want to raise goats for meat production, this chapter will equip you with the knowledge you need to capitalize on this opportunity and build a successful business.

Let's start at the beginning: the types of goat breeds considered ideal for meat:

Goat Breeds Ideal For Meat Production and Their Characteristics

Various goat breeds have been developed and recognized for their exceptional meat production capabilities.

Let's explore some popular goat breeds specifically chosen for commercial meat production and delve into the distinctive characteristics that make them ideal for meat production.

Boer Goat

The Boer goat from South Africa is an ideal breed for meat production because of its fast growth rate, excellent carcass quality, and high feed conversion efficiency, making it a preferred choice for commercial meat production.

Boer goats have a muscular build and are known for their ability to attain desirable market weights relatively quickly. Additionally, their hardiness and adaptability to various climates contribute to their popularity.

Kiko Goat

Developed in New Zealand, the Kiko goat breed has gained recognition for its exceptional meat production capabilities. Kikos exhibit strong foraging abilities, allowing them to thrive on natural vegetation and reducing the need for supplemental feed.

They have rapid growth rates and good meat conformation, producing high-quality, flavorful meat. Kikos are also known for their hardiness and disease resistance, making them suitable for extensive grazing systems.

Spanish Goat

The Spanish goat, a landrace breed, has proven its worth in commercial meat production. Spanish goats have excellent foraging abilities and can utilize available vegetation, including brush and weeds.

Although they may have smaller frames than other breeds, they compensate for this with their unique meat flavor and adaptability to harsh environmental conditions. Their hardiness, agility, and low maintenance requirements make them a practical choice for extensive production systems.

Myotonic Goat (Tennessee Fainting Goat)

The Myotonic goat, commonly called the Tennessee Fainting Goat, has characteristics that make it suitable for meat production. Despite their distinctive trait of experiencing temporary muscle stiffness when startled, fainting goats have good meat conformation and desirable carcass traits. They have a robust build and offer flavorful meat. Their manageable size and easy-going nature also contribute to their appeal in commercial settings.

Savanna Goat

Developed in South Africa, the Savanna goat has gained recognition as a breed ideal for meat production. Savannas have a strong frame, good muscling, and a rapid growth rate, resulting in desirable carcass characteristics.

They exhibit high reproductive efficiency and adaptability to various climates and management systems, making them well-suited for commercial meat production. Their hardiness and ability to thrive on diverse forage sources further contribute to their popularity.

TexMaster Goat

The TexMaster goat, a crossbreed between Boer and Tennessee Fainting goats, is a breed specifically developed for commercial meat production.

TexMasters combine Boer goats' growth rate and carcass quality with the manageable size and easy-going nature of fainting goats. They exhibit fast growth rates, excellent meat conformation, and strong maternal instincts. TexMasters are adaptable to different production systems and have proven to be successful in

Selecting Goat Meat Breeds for Profitability

As an aspiring commercial goat meat producer, selecting the right goat breed is one of the most important things you can do to be profitable. Different goat breeds have distinct characteristics that influence their growth rate, meat quality, adaptability, and profitability.

The following are some things to keep in mind when selecting goat breeds for meat production:

- **Adaptability and climate resilience**: Look for goat breeds that are well-adapted to your specific geographical region and climate conditions. Goats that can thrive in diverse environments, tolerate temperature fluctuations, and resist disease are likelier to be profitable. Consider local or indigenous breeds that have evolved to suit the local conditions.

- **Growth rate and weight gain**: Do not fail to factor in each goat breed's growth rate and weight gain potential when selecting goats for meat production. Rapid growth allows for quicker turnover and reduces the time required to bring goats to market weight. Go for breeds known for their efficient feed conversion because this will help optimize the feed-to-meat conversion ratio and minimize costs.

- **Carcass conformation and meat quality**: Evaluate the carcass conformation traits of goat breeds, including muscularity, shape, and desirable meat-to-bone ratio. Breeds with well-developed muscle mass and good meat distribution tend to produce higher-quality meat cuts that can command premium market prices.

- **Market demand and consumer preferences**: Understand the market demand and consumer preferences for goat meat in your target market. Some markets prefer specific breeds or meat characteristics, such as lean meat, while others prioritize flavor and marbling. Please research local market trends and preferences to ensure you select a breed that matches consumer demands and maximizes your chances of profitability.

- **Reproduction and fertility:** Evaluate the reproductive traits and fertility rates of different goat breeds. High fertility rates contribute to a larger number of offspring per breeding cycle, which can increase production efficiency and profitability. Consider breeds known for their reproductive performance, including early sexual maturity, high conception rates, and multiple births.

- **Maintenance and management requirements**: Consider each goat breed's maintenance and management requirements. Some breeds may have specific dietary needs, housing preferences, or health considerations. Assess feed resources, labor availability, and infrastructure requirements to ensure you choose a breed that aligns with your operational capabilities and resources.

- **Genetic selection and breeding program**: Establish a genetic selection and breeding program to improve the productivity and profitability of your herd. Identify high-performing individuals within your chosen breed and incorporate them into your breeding program to enhance desirable traits. This will help develop a genetically optimized herd that will make your goat meat production enterprise profitable.

Now you know which goat breeds are ideal for meat production and some factors to keep in mind when venturing into this business. But what about housing and infrastructure? What do you need? Let's talk about that in the next chapter:

Chapter 3: Housing and Infrastructure for Goat Meat Production

Housing and infrastructure are the foundation of successful commercial meat goat production. They provide a conducive environment for the animals' well-being, health, and productivity. Properly designed and maintained facilities ensure the goats' comfort, protection from the elements, and efficient management practices.

From sturdy shelters to secure fencing, well-designed feeding and watering systems, and appropriate handling facilities, every aspect of housing and infrastructure plays a vital role in maximizing the potential of a goat meat production unit.

Shelter Design and Layout Considerations for Meat Goats

When considering shelter design and layout, consider some key aspects to ensure your goats are comfortable, safe, and healthy enough to grow strong.

The following are some important shelter design and layout considerations for goats explicitly raised for meat production:

Space Requirements for Different Herd Sizes

The shelter should have adequate space to accommodate the number of goats in the herd.

The space requirements depend on factors such as the goats' size and breed, their age, and the purpose of the operation—in this case, meat production. Providing enough space allows for natural movement, reduces stress, and promotes social interactions among the goats.

Each goat should have enough room to lie, stand, and move comfortably. As a general guideline, aim for at least _15-20 square feet per goat_, but adjust accordingly based on the specific needs of the goats and the available space.

Ventilation and Temperature Control for Goat Comfort

Proper ventilation helps maintain good air quality and control the temperature inside the shelter.

Adequate airflow helps remove moisture, odors, and harmful gases, ensuring a healthy environment for the goats. A good shelter should have windows, vents, or eaves to facilitate fresh air exchange.

Additionally, consider natural ventilation, prevailing wind patterns, and the placement of ventilation openings to ensure proper airflow throughout the shelter.

In regions known to reach extreme temperatures, insulation and shade can help regulate the shelter's internal temperature, thus reducing heat stress and helping keep the goats comfortable.

Flooring Options for Cleanliness and Easy Maintenance

When choosing a flooring material, please pay attention to cleanliness and ease of maintenance. The flooring should be non-slippery, durable, and easy to clean.

Common flooring options include _concrete, packed dirt, or well-compacted gravel_. Concrete is the most popular choice because it is easy to clean and provides a hygienic surface.

However, if you go concrete, ensure your goats are comfortable by providing adequate bedding. Packed dirt or gravel can also be suitable, but these need regular maintenance to ensure proper drainage and cleanliness.

Fencing Requirements for Effective Containment and Security

Fencing helps you contain and secure your goats. Proper fencing helps prevent escapes, protects goats from predators, and establishes clear boundaries for grazing and movement.

The following are some important factors to consider when designing and selecting fencing options for goats specifically raised for meat production:

1. **Fence height**

The height of the fence is a crucial consideration that helps ensure your goats don't jump over or climb through.

Goats are agile animals that have a natural inclination to explore and roam. The recommendation is to have a fence height of at least 4 to 5 feet, but taller fences may be necessary for larger or more athletic goat breeds.

2. Fence strength and durability

Goats raised for meat can be strong and determined creatures, so the fencing material should be robust enough to withstand their attempts to push, lean on, or rub against it.

Woven wire fences, high-tensile electric wire, or combinations of both are the most common goat fencing material. The chosen fencing material should have adequate strength and durability to withstand the daily pressures exerted by the goats, ensuring long-term effectiveness and security.

3. Spacing and openings

The spacing between fence wires or rails should be small enough that your goats cannot squeeze through or get their heads stuck.

A spacing of _no more than 4 inches_ is generally ideal for woven wire fences, while electric fences may have different spacing requirements based on the specific design and configuration. Ensuring the spacing is appropriate to prevent escape or injury risks is important.

4. **Predator protection**

If predators are a concern in your area, the fencing design should consider measures to deter and prevent predator access.

This may involve incorporating additional features such as electric wires or netting near the ground to discourage predators from digging under the fence. Properly securing the fence to the ground can further enhance predator protection and minimize the risk of predation incidents.

5. Regular maintenance

Regular fence inspection and maintenance will help you identify and address any damage or weak areas. Goats can be naturally curious and may test the fence's strength, so prompt repairs are necessary to maintain effective containment and security. Regular maintenance should include checking for loose wires, damaged posts, or any signs of wear and tear that may compromise the fence's integrity.

6. Gates and access points

Properly designed gates and access points facilitate the movement of goats and personnel while ensuring secure entry and exit.

Gates should be sturdy, well-constructed, and wide enough that goats and maintenance equipment can pass through easily. Remember to keep the gates closed to prevent accidental escapes.

Waste Management Considerations When Raising Goats For Meat Production

Waste management is a critical aspect of goat raising that contributes to animal health, environmental sustainability, and overall farm hygiene.

The following are two key waste management considerations for meat production:

Strategies For Manure Management and Composting

Effective manure management helps minimize environmental pollution and maximizes the utilization of valuable nutrients.

Implementing regular manure removal, proper storage, and composting strategies can help manage and utilize manure effectively. You can collect and store manure in designated areas or structures, such as composting bins or pits, to allow for decomposition and nutrient breakdown.

Composting creates a favorable environment for beneficial microbes to break down organic materials, resulting in nutrient-rich compost that can be a natural fertilizer for crops or pastures.

Proper composting techniques, including adequate moisture, temperature, and aeration, should be followed to facilitate decomposition and reduce potential odor issues.

Ensuring Proper Drainage and Sanitation in the Housing Area

The design of the housing area should allow for efficient drainage of excess water and prevent stagnant water and mud accumulation. Proper grading, sloping, or using gutters and channels can promote effective water drainage.

Regularly cleaning and disinfecting the housing structures, including feeding areas, water troughs, and bedding, should minimize disease risks and maintain hygiene.

Implementing a scheduled cleaning routine and using appropriate cleaning agents and disinfectants can help control the spread of pathogens and ensure a sanitary environment for the animals.

Now that you know what to do and what to have in mind as you set up your goat structure, let's talk about feeding and nutrition:

Chapter 4: Feeding and Nutrition Requirements for Goat Meat Breeds

You will need to ace feeding and nutrition to ensure the goat you raise for meat production remain healthy and grow productively.

Goats raised for commercial goat meat production require a well-balanced diet that meets the animals' nutritional needs at different developmental stages.

Meat Goats: Considerations for Feeding and Nutrition

Let's discuss and expound on some considerations related to feeding and nutrition requirements for meat goats:

Forage and Pasture Management

A well-planned forage and pasture system ensures a consistent supply of high-quality feed for the goats.

Effective pasture management involves rotational grazing, which helps prevent overgrazing, maintain pasture health, and promote regrowth. Rotating the goats to new grazing areas allows the previously grazed pastures to recover, resulting in more productive and nutritious forage.

Energy Requirements

Your goat meat breeds need energy to maintain their growth and reproductive needs. Incorporating energy-rich feed sources into their diet is the best way to fulfill these requirements.

Grains like corn, barley, and oats are excellent energy sources you can include in the goats' feeding regimen. These grains provide concentrated energy that supports various physiological functions and promote growth.

Additionally, high-energy forages such as alfalfa can invaluably supplement the goats' energy requirements. Alfalfa is nutrient-dense and rich in high energy content, making it an excellent choice to meet the energy needs of meat goats.

By incorporating these energy-rich feed sources into their diet, meat goats can thrive and achieve optimal growth, reproduction, and overall health performance.

Protein Needs

Protein is a crucial nutrient for goats raised for meat production because it promotes muscle development, growth, and overall health. Ensuring your goats have adequate protein in their diet supports these physiological processes.

Legumes, such as alfalfa and clover, are excellent natural sources of protein that you can include in the goats' feeding program. These forages offer protein and other essential nutrients like minerals and vitamins.

Additionally, consider incorporating protein supplements into your goats' diet to ensure adequate protein provision. Common protein supplements ideal for goats include soybean meal, cottonseed meal, and canola meal. These supplements are high in protein and can help meet the goats' specific protein requirements, especially during rapid growth.

Vitamins and Minerals

While forage sources often provide a good balance of vitamins and minerals, you should also assess their nutrient content through a forage analysis. This analysis helps identify any potential deficiencies, allowing for targeted supplementation.

Common mineral supplements your goats may need include salt, calcium, phosphorus, copper, selenium, and zinc. These minerals are vital for proper bone development, muscle function, enzyme activity, and immune system support.

Vitamin supplements or fortified feeds may be necessary if the forage alone does not meet the goats' specific vitamin requirements. Vitamins A, D, and E are crucial for vision, bone health, and immune function.

Regular monitoring and consultation with a veterinarian or livestock nutritionist can help fine-tune the vitamin and mineral supplementation to meet your herds' specific needs.

Water

Adequate water intake promotes proper digestion, nutrient absorption, and overall health. Water plays a critical role in the breakdown of feed particles, allowing for efficient digestion and nutrient absorption.

Water helps maintain proper hydration, regulates body temperature, and supports the proper functioning of vital organs. Insufficient water intake can lead to dehydration, reduced feed intake, and compromised overall health. It is crucial to check water sources regularly to ensure they are clean, free from contaminants, and easily accessible to goats.

Feeding Management

Feeding practices play a crucial role in ensuring the health and well-being of your goats. One effective approach is to divide the daily feed rations into several smaller meals. This strategy optimizes digestion and prevents overconsumption, allowing the goats to process the nutrients efficiently without overwhelming their digestive system.

Additionally, it is important to use feeders that minimize waste, spoilage, and competition for feed. These feeders help maintain a clean and hygienic feeding environment, reducing unnecessary expenses and ensuring all goats have equal access to their required feed. Furthermore, adjust the feed intake based on individual goat requirements and regularly monitor their body condition scores.

When you have proper housing and a dialed-in feeding routine, your goats will flourish, and you will reap the benefits.

In the next chapter, we shall focus on how to scale your goat meat production enterprise.

Chapter 5: Scaling and Expanding A Goat Meat Production Business

As demand for meat products grows, businesses in this industry must strategically plan their expansion to meet market needs and increase profitability.

Successful scaling requires a comprehensive approach that encompasses various aspects of the operation. Implementing well-defined strategies and adapting to market dynamics allows meat producers to navigate the complexities of growth and position themselves for long-term success in the competitive meat industry.

Below are some key considerations that'll help you scale and expand your enterprise:

Strategic Ways to Expand Your Herd And Production Capacity

These strategies may involve acquiring additional land for grazing or constructing new barns and shelters to accommodate more animals. Before you do any of that, assess the availability of resources like feed, water, and pasture to ensure sustainable growth.

Implementing efficient breeding and reproduction programs can help increase the number of animals in the herd. Working with veterinarians and animal nutritionists can provide valuable insights into optimizing animal health and performance.

Identifying Opportunities for Value-Added Meat Products

Diversifying the product range and exploring value-added meat products can create new opportunities for growth and increased profitability. This may involve exploring options like processing meat into various cuts, sausages, jerky, or smoked meats.

Additionally, getting into niche markets or specialty products, such as organic or grass-fed meat, can help differentiate the business and tap into specific consumer preferences.

Market research and understanding consumer trends can help you develop value-added products.

Collaborating with Local Processors and Distributors

Partnering with local processors and distributors can expand your market reach and streamline operations. Collaborating with reputable processors can help ensure efficient meat processing and packaging, maintain quality standards, and meet regulatory requirements.

Building strong relationships with distributors and retailers can help expand distribution channels and reach a wider customer base. This collaboration can also provide access to valuable market insights and help you penetrate new markets and regions.

Managing the Logistics of Transportation and Supply Chain

As the business expands, effective logistics management becomes crucial. This includes managing transportation logistics to ensure timely and efficient delivery of products to customers.

Optimizing supply chain management involves coordinating with suppliers, monitoring inventory levels, and ensuring consistent availability of inputs such as feed and medication.

Implementing proper record-keeping systems and utilizing technology-based solutions can streamline logistics processes and promote real-time inventory and supply chain activity monitoring.

Financial Planning

Scaling up and expanding the business requires careful financial planning. Start by assessing the capital requirements for infrastructure development, herd expansion, and equipment purchases.

From there, develop a comprehensive business plan, including projected financials and cash flow analysis, to ensure you can secure funding from banks, investors, or government programs. Engaging with financial advisors or agricultural specialists can provide valuable guidance in financial planning and accessing the necessary funds for expansion.

The various things discussed in this section should help you start a successful goat meat-raising enterprise.

In the next section, we shall focus on how to start raising goats for commercial milk production:

Section 2

How to Raise Goats For Commercial Milk Production

Chapter 6: Introduction to Commercial Goat Milk Production

Raising goats for commercial milk production involves systematically and efficiently managing dairy goats to maximize milk yields and quality.

It is a profitable venture that requires careful planning, proper breed selection, appropriate feeding and nutrition, and suitable housing and infrastructure. By focusing on these key aspects, dairy goat farmers can establish a successful business that meets market demand for high-quality milk and milk products.

If you'd like to get into this business as a beginner, breed selection is the first thing you need to know about and ace, so let's focus on that:

Popular Goat Breeds For Milk Production and Their Characteristics

When selecting dairy goat breeds for high milk yields, you should consider several factors, including the breed's reputation for milk production, genetic potential, adaptability to local conditions, and personal preferences.

The following are a few dairy goat breeds known for their high milk yields:

Alpine

Alpines are medium to large-sized goats known for their high milk production. They have a calm and friendly temperament and adapt well to various climates. Alpines have excellent udder development, contributing to their impressive milk yields.

They can produce an average of 2,000 to 3,000 pounds of milk annually. The milk produced by Alpines has a butterfat content ranging from 3% to 4%, making it suitable for a variety of dairy products.

Alpines are also valued for their hardiness and adaptability, making them ideal for different management systems and environments.

Saanen

Saanens are known for their exceptional milk production and are often called the "Holsteins of the dairy goat world." They have a calm and gentle temperament, which makes them easy to handle and manage.

Saanens can produce large quantities of milk, with some nannies yielding over 3,000 pounds annually. The milk has a butterfat content of around 3% to 4%, making it suitable for a range of dairy products.

Toggenburg

Toggenburgs are medium-sized goats that originated in Switzerland. They have a distinctive brown color with white markings on their face and legs. Toggenburgs are known for their adaptability to different climates and ability to thrive in rugged terrain.

They are reliable milk producers, producing an average of 2,000 to 3,000 pounds annually. The milk of Toggenburgs has a butterfat content of around 3% to 4%. They are also famous for their longevity and disease resistance, making them popular among dairy goat farmers.

Nubian

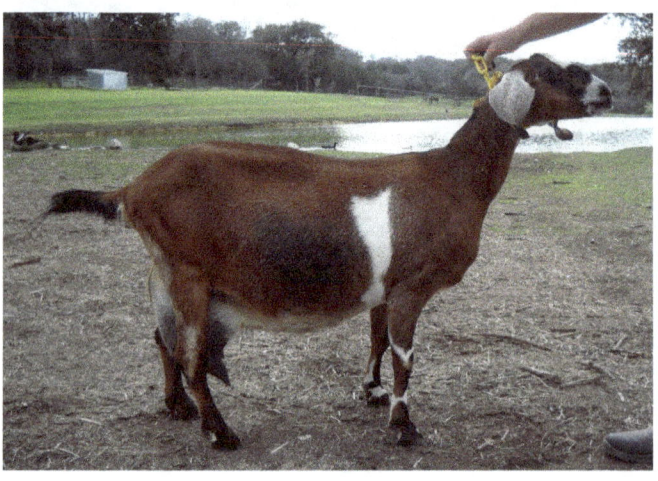

Nubians are known for the high butterfat content in their milk, ranging from 4% to 5%.

Nubians produce milk with a rich and creamy texture, making it ideal for cheese and butter production. They are reliable milk producers, with average yearly yields of around 1,800 to

2,800 pounds. Nubians are also friendly and sociable, making them popular as dairy goats and pets.

LaMancha

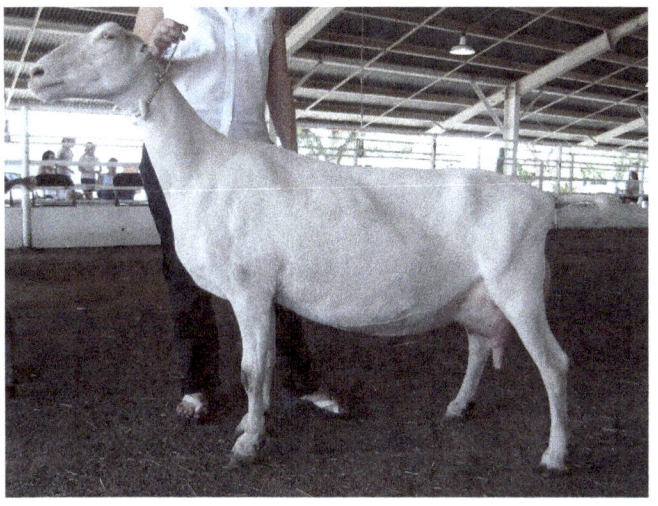

LaManchas are a unique breed known for their short ears, sometimes called "gopher ears."

LaManchas have a calm and gentle temperament, making them easy to handle and work with. They are reliable milk producers, with average yearly yields ranging from 1,800 to 2,200 pounds. The milk of LaManchas has a butterfat content of around 3% to 4%.

Due to their compact size and friendly disposition, LaManchas are also popular as 4-H project animals and for small-scale dairy operations.

Oberhasli

Oberhaslis have a gentle temperament and adapt well to different environments. Oberhaslis are good milk producers, with average yearly yields ranging from 1,800 to 2,500 pounds. The milk of Oberhaslis has a butterfat content of around 3% to 4%.

They are also known for their efficiency in converting feed into milk, making them an economical choice for dairy goat farmers.

Nigerian Dwarf

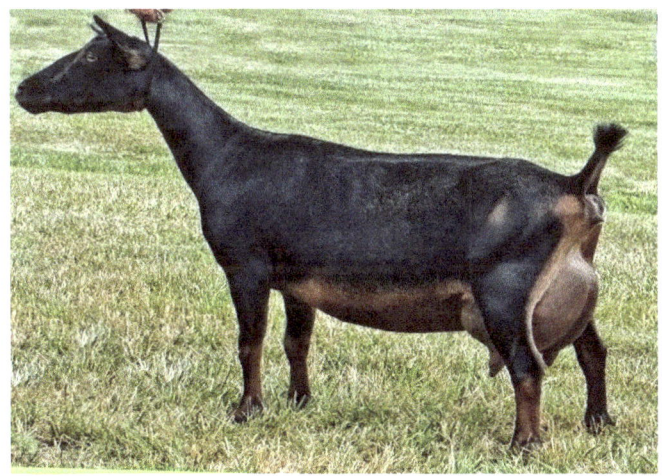

Nigerian Dwarf goats are small-sized goats popular for milk production and as pets. Despite their size, they are good milk producers, with average yields ranging from 600 to 1,200 pounds per year. Nigerian Dwarf goats produce milk with a high butterfat content of around 6% to 10%, making it exceptionally rich and flavorful.

These popular goat milk breeds offer a range of options for dairy farmers, homesteaders, and enthusiasts looking to enjoy the benefits of goat milk. Each breed has unique characteristics and qualities, allowing you to choose based on your needs, preferences, and farming conditions.

Factors to Consider When Selecting Goat Breeds for Profitable Milk Production

When selecting goat breeds for profitable milk production, keep the following factors in mind:

- **Milk yield**: This is the quantity of milk a goat breed produces. Higher milk yield directly impacts profitability since more milk means you can sell more milk or process it into value-added products. Look for breeds known for their high average daily milk production and lactation length.

- **Fat and protein content**: Consumers often prefer goat milk with higher fat and protein percentages; milk with higher fat and protein content can also command a higher price in the market. Breeds consistently producing milk with higher fat and protein content can increase profitability.

- **Feed efficiency**: Feed efficiency is a goat's ability to convert feed into milk. Breeds that effectively utilize feed can help reduce feed costs and increase profitability. Go for breeds known for their feed efficiency because they require less feed to produce a certain amount of milk.

- **Adaptability**: Some goat breeds are better suited for specific climates, terrain, or management systems. Consider factors such as heat tolerance, cold tolerance, parasite resistance, and forage adaptability. Select a breed that can thrive in your environmental conditions to minimize health issues and maximize milk production.

- **Health and disease resistance**: You cannot run a commercially successful goat milk production unit if your goats are unhealthy. Look for breeds with a reputation for being hardy and resilient, with good overall health and disease resistance. Goats resistant to common diseases prevalent in your area will require fewer veterinary interventions, reducing potential expenses.

- **Market demand**: Research the local or regional market to understand consumer preferences, cultural preferences, and the availability of processing facilities for specific goat milk products. Look for breeds that produce milk sought after in your target market. Consider taste preferences, texture, and specific uses (e.g., cheese making, yogurt production) to align your breed selection with market demand.

Remember that breed selection is not solely about determining profitability; market dynamics, input costs, management practices, and marketing strategies also influence your choice.

Therefore, thorough research, consulting experienced breeders, and carefully evaluating your situation will help you make informed decisions when selecting goat breeds for profitable milk production.

As you start commercial goat milk production, you must set up housing and other infrastructure for your milk production herd.

Let's talk about this in the next chapter.

Chapter 6: Housing and Infrastructure for Milk Production

Housing and infrastructure are vital because they ensure dairy goats have a comfortable and productive environment. Proper facilities ensure the animals' well-being, facilitate efficient milking routines and help maintain milk quality.

Let's explore housing and infrastructure requirements for commercial goat milk production:

Shelter and Barns

Shelters and barns are key housing infrastructure necessary for goat milk production. They protect goats from adverse weather conditions and contribute to operational success.

Here is a more detailed exploration of shelter and barn requirements:

Structure and Design

The shelter or barn should be well-constructed with sturdy materials to ensure durability and longevity. It should provide adequate space for each goat to move around comfortably and lie down.

Using materials that are easy to clean and sanitize, such as concrete, metal, or high-quality wood, can make a lot of difference. Also, install proper insulation to regulate temperature and provide a comfortable environment for the goats throughout the year.

Ventilation

Good ventilation maintains air quality, prevents the buildup of moisture and harmful gases, and promotes goats' health.

Strategically installing windows, vents, or fans can facilitate fresh air exchange and remove stale air. Proper airflow helps control humidity levels, reduces the risk of respiratory diseases, and keeps the goats comfortable.

Flooring

The flooring should be non-slip, comfortable, and easy to clean and disinfect. Concrete flooring is the most commonly used because it is durable, smooth, and easy to clean. Providing bedding, such as straw or wood shavings, can enhance comfort and moisture absorption.

Lighting

Sufficient lighting in the shelter or barn creates a well-lit environment for the goats and facilitates management tasks.

Natural lighting is ideal, so design the structure with windows or skylights to maximize daylight. Supplementing with artificial lighting when needed, especially during darker months or for extended daylight hours, can ensure adequate lighting.

Separation and Partitioning

Divide the shelter or barn into separate areas, such as sleeping areas, feeding areas, and kidding or maternity pens. Installing sturdy partitions or gates allows for easy separation and management of goats based on their needs or stages of production.

Hygiene and Sanitation

Regularly removing manure and soiled bedding helps prevent the buildup of bacteria and parasites. Clean and disinfect the shelter or barn periodically, and pay attention to feeders, water troughs, and other equipment.

Milking Parlor Setup

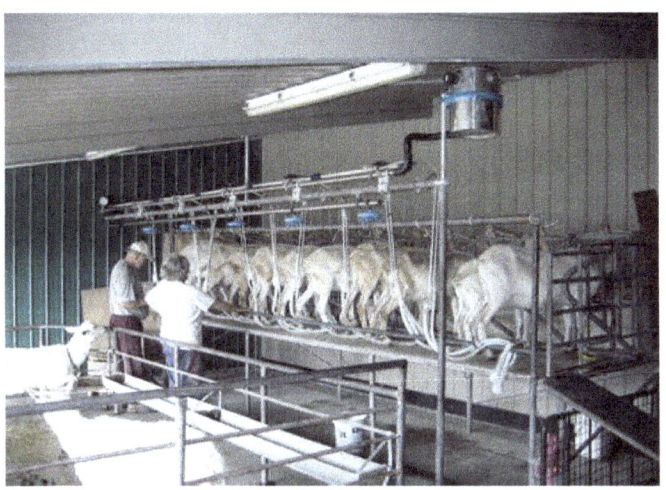

A milking parlor setup is critical to dairy goat farming and commercial milk production. It involves designing and organizing a dedicated space that makes milking the goats easier, more efficient, and hygienic.

A well-designed milking parlor ensures the comfort of the goats, facilitates smooth milking operations, and helps maintain milk quality.

Let's look a bit deeper into setting up a milking parlor:

Layout and Design

First, carefully plan the layout to optimize workflow, ensuring a smooth and organized process for the goats and milkers.

Considerations include the number of goats you want to milk simultaneously and the available space within the milking area.

The design of the milking parlor can vary, such as herringbone, parallel, or rotary systems, depending on the farm's specific needs and resources.

Each design has advantages and considerations, including efficiency, labor requirements, and space utilization.

The chosen layout should prioritize ease of movement for the goats and milkers, allowing for comfortable access to the udders and ensuring minimal animal stress.

Milking Equipment

Milking equipment is crucial in efficient and hygienic milk extraction from dairy goats. Selecting and maintaining appropriate milking equipment is important to ensure optimal milk production and quality. Here is a detailed exploration of milking equipment in dairy goat farming:

1. **<u>Milking machines</u>**

Milking machines are invaluable tools because they offer a streamlined and efficient approach to milking.

When selecting milking machines, opt for models explicitly designed for dairy goats because goats' udder size and shape differ from other dairy animals. This ensures a proper fit and optimal milking experience.

The milking machines should have appropriate pulsation settings that mimic the natural sucking action of a kid, which promotes milk let-down and prevents any potential harm or discomfort to the goats.

Furthermore, ensure that the teat cups fit snugly onto the goat's teats to create a secure seal that prevents air leaks during the milking process. This tight seal enhances milk extraction efficiency and minimizes the risk of contamination.

2. Vacuum system

The vacuum system is a vital milking equipment component because it generates the necessary suction to extract milk from the goat's udder. Maintaining the vacuum level within the recommended range ensures the comfort and well-being of the goats during milking.

Regularly checking and calibrating the vacuum system ensures consistent and appropriate suction pressure. This helps optimize milk flow and extraction efficiency.

A reliable vacuum pump helps maintain the required vacuum levels throughout the milking process. By properly managing the vacuum system, dairy goat farmers can ensure gentle and effective milk extraction, promoting their goats' overall health and welfare.

3. <u>Milk storage and transfer equipment</u>

Choose suitable equipment that is easy to clean, sanitize, and maintain, thus ensuring milk quality and hygiene. Common options include stainless steel milk cans or bulk tanks, depending on the scale of the operation. When selecting the storage capacity, consider the size of the herd and expected milk production to ensure adequate storage space.

Transferring milk from the storage equipment to designated processing or cooling areas is another key step. You can streamline this process by using food-grade transfer pumps or pipelines to maintain the integrity and safety of the milk.

4. **Monitoring and automation systems**

Monitoring and automation systems offer valuable tools that enhance efficiency and milk production in dairy goat farming. Consider integrating these systems into milking equipment to optimize operations. Automated cluster removal systems can streamline the milking process by automatically removing the milking unit after milking, which reduces labor and improves efficiency.

Milk flow sensors or meters provide real-time data on individual goat yields and milk quality parameters, allowing for accurate production monitoring and assessment. These systems enable timely identification of any issues or abnormalities, such as low milk flow or changes in milk quality, during milking, which facilitates prompt intervention and optimal milk production.

Sanitary Conditions

Dairy goat farmers should implement robust hygiene protocols to uphold cleanliness and sanitation standards. Regularly clean and sanitize all milking equipment, surfaces, and utensils to remove potential contaminants and maintain a hygienic environment.

Provide adequate handwashing facilities for milkers and enforce proper milker hygiene practices, such as wearing clean clothing and disposable gloves. Milk is highly susceptible to bacterial contamination; maintaining sanitary conditions minimizes the risk of milk-borne diseases and ensures the final product is safe for human consumption.

Udder Preparation

Prioritize udder cleanliness before milking. Consider implementing a pre-milking routine that includes thorough udder cleaning and gentle stimulation to promote milk let-down and improve milk flow.

Cleaning the udder helps remove dirt, debris, and potential pathogens that could contaminate the milk.

It is important to use approved udder sanitizing agents to minimize the risk of bacterial contamination.

These sanitizing agents help kill bacteria on the udder's surface, reducing the chances of milk-borne infections.

Record Keeping

Maintain accurate milk production records, including individual goat yields, milk quality parameters, and milking times.

By documenting this information, you can gain valuable insights into the performance of your goats, identify trends, and make informed decisions regarding breeding, feeding, and management practices.

Implementing appropriate record-keeping systems, such as computerized data management software or manual logbooks, ensures you have organized and systematic milking data. These records provide a historical reference for future analysis, evaluation, and comparison.

Waste Management

Effective waste management practices help maintain a clean and hygienic environment, reduce environmental pollution, and promote sustainable farming. Waster management includes managing goat manure by collecting it regularly, composting it for nutrient-rich fertilizer, and utilizing it for crop production.

Proper bedding management ensures a comfortable and clean-living environment for the goats, while effluent management involves capturing and treating liquid waste from cleaning processes. Solid waste, such as packaging materials, should be recycled or disposed of properly.

Odor control measures help minimize odors and maintain a pleasant working and living environment. Compliance with local regulations regarding waste management is essential to meet legal requirements and protect the environment.

Chapter 7: Feeding and Nutrition Requirements for Dairy Goats

Feeding and nutrition requirements are crucial to managing a successful dairy goat farm. Proper nutrition maximizes milk production, maintains good health, and promotes productivity.

Considerations for Feeding and Nutrition Requirements

Consider the following core things to ensure your dairy goats remain well-fed.

Forage and Roughage

Forage and roughage are the primary sources of fiber, essential nutrients and promote rumen health. Forage options such as pasture, hay, and silage should be abundant and high-quality, free from mold, dust, and harmful plants.

Making various forage options available to your goats ensures a balanced and diverse diet that meets their nutritional needs. It also stimulates their appetite and helps maintain a healthy rumen environment.

Stock forage availability and quality monitoring can help ensure your dairy goats receive adequate nutrition. From there, you can adjust supplementation based on the availability and quality of forage, ensuring optimal nutrition and promoting the overall well-being of dairy goats.

Concentrates and Supplements

Concentrates and supplements are crucial to a dairy goat's diet because they provide additional nutrients and support optimal milk production. These concentrates include grains, protein sources, and mineral supplements.

It is essential to develop a balanced ration that meets the specific nutritional needs of dairy goats, providing adequate energy, protein, vitamins, and minerals. Working closely with a nutritionist or veterinarian can ensure you formulate a diet tailored to the herd's requirements and production goals.

When introducing concentrates, it is important to allow the goats' digestive systems to adjust gradually, which also prevents digestive upsets.

Protein Requirements

Dairy goats have high protein requirements, particularly during the lactation period. It is important to incorporate protein-rich feeds into their diet to meet these requirements.

Excellent protein sources include soybean, canola, and alfalfa, which provide essential amino acids for milk synthesis and muscle development. Do not forget to monitor protein levels in the ration to avoid excessive or deficient intake.

Excessive protein intake can lead to inefficient nutrient use, increased ammonia production, and potential health issues. On the other hand, inadequate protein intake can result in reduced milk production and compromised overall health.

Energy Sources

Energy-dense feeds such as grains like corn, barley, and oats and oilseeds such as soybeans and sunflower seeds provide the necessary fuel for milk synthesis. However, please balance these energy sources with a good fiber content to maintain a healthy rumen environment. Fiber-rich feeds, such as high-quality forage, help stimulate rumination and maintain proper rumen function.

Adjust energy levels in the diet based on factors such as the stage of lactation, body condition, and specific milk production goals. This ensures that the goats receive the right amount of energy to support their metabolic demands and milk production without excessive fat deposition or inadequate energy supply.

Mineral and Vitamin Supplementation

Key minerals include calcium, phosphorus, magnesium, copper, and zinc. In contrast, essential vitamins include A, D, and E. Offering a free-choice mineral supplement specifically formulated for dairy goats allows them to regulate their intake based on their needs. Regular testing forage and water sources can help you identify deficiencies or imbalances in mineral and vitamin content.

Based on the test results, you can adjust the supplementation regimen to address any specific deficiencies or imbalances to ensure your dairy goats receive the necessary nutrients for optimal health, reproduction, and milk production.

We cannot talk about running a successful dairy goat farm and fail to mention milk processing and value-added products.

Let's do that in the next chapter:

Chapter 8: Milk Processing and Value Addition

Milk processing transforms raw milk into value-added products. This chapter explores the importance of milk processing, focusing on enhancing milk's shelf life, safety, and versatility. You can enhance goat milk's usability using various processing methods and take various goat products to the market.

Ensuring Milk Safety: Pasteurization

A key objective of milk processing is to ensure safety by eliminating harmful bacteria and pathogens. The method usually used to achieve this is pasteurization.

Pasteurization involves heating milk to a specific temperature and then holding that temp for a predetermined time to kill potential microorganisms. This process reduces the risk of foodborne illnesses and preserves the milk's nutritional quality.

Value-Added Products: Milk Powder

After pasteurization, we can process milk into a wide range of value-added products. One such product is milk powder, which we obtain by removing the water content in milk.

Milk powder offers an extended shelf life and is convenient for storage and transportation. It finds application in various products such as infant formula, bakery goods, and as a base for beverages.

Value-Added Products: Cheese

Cheese production is another popular value-added product in the dairy industry. It involves curdling the milk, separating the curds from the whey, and subjecting them to further processing techniques such as pressing, aging, and flavoring.

You can produce different types of cheese, each with its unique texture, flavor, and characteristics. Cheese is a versatile ingredient consumed or used in cooking, usually to add richness and depth to various dishes.

Value-Added Products: Yogurt

Yogurt is a widely consumed value-added product derived from milk processing. The yogurt-production process involves fermenting milk with specific bacterial cultures that convert lactose into lactic acid, resulting in a thickened and tangy product.

Yogurt is popular and well-liked for its probiotic properties that provide beneficial bacteria for gut health. It is available in various flavors, and many people consume it as a standalone snack, in smoothies, or in recipes as a healthier alternative to cream or sour cream.

Value-Added Products: Butter and Cream

Butter and cream are popular dairy products obtained through milk processing.

Butter comes from churning cream until the fat molecules cluster together, separating from the buttermilk. It serves as a spread, cooking ingredient, and baking ingredient.

Conversely, the cream can be used as a standalone ingredient, whipped into a fluffy texture, or incorporated into sauces and desserts.

Specialized Products: Lactose-Free Milk, Flavored Milk, and Enriched Milk

Milk processing also produces specialized products that cater to specific dietary needs and preferences.

For example, lactose-free milk undergoes lactose removal to make it suitable for individuals with lactose intolerance. Flavored milk offers a variety of tastes, appealing to different consumer preferences. Enriched milk is fortified with added vitamins and minerals, providing enhanced nutritional benefits.

Processing goat milk into these value-added products may require special infrastructural provisions. If you want to venture into these products, do your due diligence, research your market, and consult professionals who can guide you.

Section 3

How to Raise Goats For Commercial Fiber Production

Chapter 9: Introduction to Raising Goats for Fiber Production

Raising goats for commercial fiber production involves cultivating and harvesting high-quality fibers from goats for various textile and fiber-based industries.

This specialized aspect of goat farming requires careful breed selection, proper feeding and nutrition, suitable housing and infrastructure, and efficient shearing and fiber processing techniques.

This section will examine the different aspects of raising goats for commercial fiber production and provide insights into establishing and managing a successful commercial enterprise that produces goat fiber.

Popular Fiber-Producing Goat Breeds and Their Characteristics

Humans have valued goats for their fiber-producing capabilities for centuries. From luxurious cashmere to durable mohair, goat fibers offer a wide range of qualities and applications in the textile industry.

Let's discuss a few of these remarkable animals and the valuable fibers they provide.

Cashmere Goats

Cashmere goats are renowned for producing one of the world's most luxurious and sought-after fibers.

Originating from the harsh climates of Central Asia, cashmere goats have adapted to survive in extreme cold. The cashmere fiber they produce is incredibly soft, lightweight, and insulating.

Cashmere goats have a double coat, with coarse outer guard hair and a fine undercoat, which is the source of the prized cashmere fiber. We typically collect the undercoat through combing or shearing.

Angora Coats

Angora goats are famous for their mohair fiber, which many value for its luster, resilience, and versatility. First bred in Turkey, these goats are now available worldwide.

Mohair is a durable and lustrous fiber known for its exceptional dye absorption and ability to blend with other fibers. Angora goats have a thick, curly, dense fleece that requires regular shearing.

Pygora Goats

Pygora goats are a relatively newer breed developed by crossing Angora and Pygmy goats. They combine the fine and soft fiber qualities of Angora goats with the hardiness and ease of care of Pygmy goats.

Pygora fiber is highly versatile and comes in three distinct types: Type A (Mohair-like), Type B (Cashmere-like), and Type C (A blend of both). Pygora goats are small, making them suitable for small-scale fiber production and ideal for hobbyists and small farms.

Nigora Goats

Nigora goats are a crossbreed between Nigerian Dwarf and Angora goats.

These goats produce a fiber that combines cashmere's softness with mohair's luster and strength. Nigora fiber is highly prized for its unique characteristics and often blends well with other fibers to enhance their properties. These goats are known for their friendly temperament and are an excellent choice for fiber production.

It's important to note that fiber quality can vary within each breed, and management and nutrition usually determine the fiber quality produced.

Factors to Consider When Selecting Goat Breeds for Fiber Production

When selecting a fiber-producing goat breed, you should consider various factors that will help you choose one that aligns with your goals, resources, and preferences.

Listed below are some key factors to consider:

- **Fiber quality:** Different goat breeds produce fibers with varying characteristics, such as the sumptuously soft cashmere, the resilient and lustrous mohair, or even a blend of both. Evaluating the fiber's softness, luster, strength, and versatility lets you determine if it aligns with your desired standards and intended use.

- **Climate adaptability:** It is essential to evaluate the climate and environmental conditions in your location to ensure the well-being and productivity of the goats. Different breeds have varying levels of adaptability to specific climates. For example, cashmere goats are well-suited for cold climates because they have developed the ability to thrive in harsh and frigid conditions. On the other hand, breeds like Angora goats exhibit a wider tolerance range, making them adaptable to various temperatures.

- **Care and maintenance:** Each breed has specific care requirements, and it's crucial to assess the time, effort, and resources you can dedicate to goat care. Consider grooming, shearing frequency, feeding requirements, and general health maintenance before settling on a specific breed. Some breeds may demand more attention and specialized care than others, requiring regular grooming to prevent matting or higher shearing frequency due to faster fiber growth.

- **Production scale and purpose:** Determine the scale of your fiber production operation. If you have a small farm or are a hobbyist, breeds like Pygora or Nigora goats might be more suitable. However, if you want a large-scale production, opt for breeds that offer higher fiber yields, such as specialized cashmere or mohair breeds.

Besides the breed, running a commercially successful goat fiber-producing business requires structures and specific infrastructure.

Let's talk about that in the next chapter:

Chapter 10: Housing and Infrastructure for Goat Fiber Production

Housing and infrastructure are crucial in successful goat fiber production; they ensure the goats' well-being and facilitate efficient fiber management. Properly designed and maintained facilities provide a comfortable and safe environment for the goats, protect the fiber quality, and support the operation's overall productivity.

Here are the various structures you need for operational efficiency:

Shearing and Fiber Processing Facilities

Setting up shearing and fiber processing facilities requires careful planning and attention to detail.

The following examples describe what these facilities should entail:

Shearing Area

A well-designed shearing area should prioritize cleanliness, with surfaces that are easy to sanitize and maintain. Adequate lighting lets shearers see the goats' fiber and perform precise shearing. Proper ventilation ensures good air circulation, reducing the buildup of dust and heat that can be discomforting to the goats and shearers.

The flooring should be non-slippery to prevent accidents and injuries and be easy to clean to maintain hygiene standards. Secure restraining equipment such as stocks or shearing stands should be available to immobilize the goats and safely facilitate efficient shearing. This ensures the goats' well-being during the process and contributes to the overall efficiency and effectiveness of the shearing operation.

Shearing Equipment

Invest in high-quality shearing equipment to ensure a successful fiber production operation. Choose shearing equipment based on the type of fiber you will harvest from your goats. These tools efficiently remove the fiber while minimizing the risk of injury to the goats and the shearers.

The following are some essential tools commonly used for goat shearing:

1. **Shears**

Electric or manual shears are the primary tools used to shave goats. Because electric shears are electricity or battery-powered, they provide faster and more efficient shearing.

In contrast, manual shears require physical force to operate and are suitable for smaller flocks or areas with limited or no access to electricity.

2. **Combs and cutters**

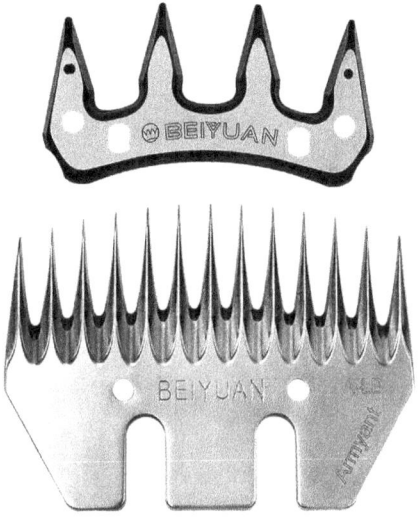

Combs and cutters are attachments fitted onto the shears.

They come in various sizes and configurations that cater to the desired cut length and the type of fiber being shorn. Combs have teeth that hold the fiber while the cutters slice through it.

3. **Blade sharpening tools**

Regularly maintaining shearing equipment ensures optimal performance. Blade sharpening tools maintain sharpness and ensure clean and precise cuts.

4. **Protective gear**

Shearers should use appropriate protective gear to ensure safety during shearing. This may include shearing smocks or coveralls, gloves, safety glasses, and sturdy footwear.

Investing in high-quality shearing equipment and regularly maintaining it ensures efficient shearing, minimizes goats' stress, and produces high-quality fiber. Proper training in using and maintaining the equipment is also essential to ensure safe and effective shearing practices.

Fiber Processing Facilities

Fiber processing facilities transform raw fiber into market-ready products. These facilities encompass various areas and equipment for sorting, cleaning, and packaging fiber.

The following are the three main structures you need to establish an effective fiber processing facility:

1. **Sorting area**

A dedicated sorting area helps assess the quality and characteristics of the fiber. This area should provide ample space to spread the fiber and allow easy visual inspection.

This space should be well-lit, clean, and organized to ensure workers can efficiently sort the fiber based on its quality, color, length, and other relevant attributes. Proper organization and labeling of sorting bins or containers can help maintain order and facilitate accurate inventory management.

2. __Cleaning facilities__

Cleaning the fiber removes impurities and prepares the goat fiber for further processing or packaging. Different equipment, such as drum carders, picker machines, or dehairing equipment, can help with this endeavor, so choose what you need depending on the specific fiber type.

For example, drum carders are an effective way to card and align fibers, while picker machines help separate and open the fibers. Dehairing equipment removes coarse or unwanted fibers from the finer ones.

3. **Packaging stations**

After sorting and cleaning the fiber, the next step is properly packaging it for storage or sale.

Packaging stations should be well-organized and equipped with appropriate materials, such as storage bags, boxes, or containers, to preserve the fiber's quality and protect it from moisture, dust, and pests. Clearly labeled packaging helps identify fiber types, grades, or colors for easy inventory management and marketing.

Storage and Marketing

Storing and marketing fiber products is integral to a successful commercial fiber production operation. Proper storage preserves the quality and value of the harvested fibers, while effective marketing helps generate sales and create a demand for fiber products.

Let's explore each aspect in detail below:

Storage

Adequate storage facilities will protect the fibers from environmental factors that can damage their quality. The storage area should be dry, well-ventilated, and free from pests or rodents.

Store goat fibers in containers or bags that offer protection from moisture, dust, and sunlight. Also, organize the storage area and label everything to facilitate easy access and inventory management. Conduct regular maintenance to identify and address potential issues affecting the fibers' integrity.

Marketing

You can explore various marketing channels to reach your target customers. These can include online platforms, such as ecommerce websites or social media platforms, where you can showcase your products and engage with potential buyers.

Participating in fiber festivals, trade shows, and local markets is a great way to interact directly with customers and showcase the uniqueness of fiber products. Collaborating with fiber processors, textile manufacturers, and artisans can help establish valuable partnerships that expand marketing reach and access to new markets.

Highlighting the unique characteristics of the fibers, such as their softness, luster, and sustainability, can be a compelling selling point. Using high-quality product imagery and clear product descriptions helps attract potential customers and communicate the value of fiber products. Offering samples or small-scale trial packs can allow customers to experience the quality firsthand, potentially leading to larger orders.

Building a strong online presence through a dedicated website or social media platforms is another great way to connect with fiber enthusiasts, yarn shops, and textile designers. Engaging with the fiber community through educational content, blog posts, or tutorials can help build brand loyalty and establish the farmer as an expert.

Maintaining good customer relationships is crucial for repeat business and positive word-of-mouth referrals. Providing excellent customer service, promptly addressing inquiries or concerns, and ensuring timely delivery of orders contribute to a positive customer experience.

By focusing on effective storage practices and implementing a well-planned marketing strategy, you can maximize the value of your fiber products and establish a strong presence in the market. Combining high-quality fibers with effective marketing efforts will help attract customers, build a loyal customer base, and ultimately drive the success of the commercial fiber production venture.

Chapter 11: Feeding and Nutrition Requirements for Fiber Goats

Feeding and nutritional requirements play a crucial role in maintaining health and promoting the growth of fiber goats. Proper nutrition ensures the production of high-quality fibers with desirable characteristics.

Considerations for Feeding and Nutrition Requirements

Let's delve into the key aspects of feeding and nutrition requirements for fiber goats:

Forage and Roughage

Forage and roughage play a vital role in the nutrition and well-being of fiber goats. These fiber-rich feeds, including pasture, hay, and forage crops, serve as the primary source of nutrients for these animals.

Access to high-quality provides essential fibers, vitamins, and minerals necessary for optimal digestion and overall health and ensures the goats produce high-quality fibers.

It is important to select and manage the forage carefully to ensure its quality and that it's free from molds, harmful plants, and contaminants that can negatively affect the goats' health.

Fiber-Specific Concentrates

Fiber-specific concentrates can help meet the nutritional requirements of fiber goats and promote optimal fiber growth and health. These specialized feeds use a special formulation that provides essential nutrients that support the development of strong, fine, and lustrous fibers.

Fiber goat feeds typically have higher levels of fiber and lower levels of carbohydrates than feeds for other goats. This nutrient composition ensures that fiber goats receive the necessary building blocks for robust fiber production while minimizing excessive energy intake that could lead to undesirable weight gain.

Protein Requirements

Meeting the protein requirements of fiber goats supports optimal fiber growth, overall health, and body condition. Including protein-rich sources in their diet, such as soybean, canola, or alfalfa, ensures an adequate intake of essential amino acids necessary for fiber development.

Protein helps synthesize keratin, the main component of fibers, which contributes to their strength and quality.

Additionally, sufficient protein intake supports a healthy immune system and promotes proper body condition, allowing goats to thrive in fiber-producing roles.

Mineral and Vitamin Supplementation

Minerals such as copper, zinc, selenium, and manganese are crucial to goat fiber development because they ensure the fibers are strong, elastic, and high-quality. Vitamin supplementation, including vitamins A, D, and E, helps the goats maintain a robust immune system that supports optimal fiber growth.

Regular forage and water sources testing helps identify mineral or vitamin deficiencies or imbalances. By pinpointing specific nutritional needs through testing, you can implement targeted supplementation to address any shortcomings and ensure fiber goats receive the necessary minerals and vitamins to thrive.

Chapter 12: Fiber Processing and Value-Addition

Value addition refers to transforming raw fiber into higher-value products. By adding value to their fiber, goat farmers can maximize their profits and expand their market opportunities.

Listed below are some ways to add value to fiber goats:

- **Fiber processing**: One of the primary value-addition methods is processing raw fiber into finished products. This can include carding, spinning, weaving, or felting the fibers to create yarns, fabrics, garments, or other textile products. You can learn these skills or collaborate with skilled fiber processors or artisans capable of converting raw fiber into marketable products.

- **Fiber blending**: Different fibers, such as goat fiber and other natural fibers like wool or silk, can create unique blends with enhanced characteristics. Fiber blending allows farmers to create yarns or fabrics with improved softness, strength, or color variations, increasing the market appeal of their products.

- **Dyeing and color enhancement**: Dyeing the fiber or using natural methods to enhance its color can add value and increase the aesthetic appeal of the final product. Goat farmers can experiment with natural dyes, such as plant-based or insect-derived dyes, to create diverse colors and patterns in their fiber products.

- **Product development**: Developing value-added products beyond raw fiber can expand market opportunities. This can include creating finished garments, accessories, home decor items, or even specialty products like luxury fiber blends or handcrafted items. Goat farmers can collaborate with local designers or artisans to create unique, high-quality products that cater to specific market demands.

- **Education and workshops**: Offering educational programs, workshops, or tours on fiber production, processing, or fiber arts can attract enthusiasts and create additional revenue streams. Sharing knowledge and expertise with others can generate income and raise awareness about fiber goat products' value and versatility.

By adding value to their fiber through processing, goat farmers can tap into niche markets, command higher prices, and establish a reputation for having premium products.

Chapter 13: Commercial Goat Breeding

Breeding operations are an integral part of the livestock industry that is crucial to meeting the growing demand for goat meat, dairy products, and fiber. These operations seek to maximize productivity, genetic improvement, and profitability by employing various breeding strategies and management practices.

Let's delve into the key aspects of commercial goat breeding operations:

- **Breeding objectives**: Commercial breeding operations have specific goals and objectives. These goals may include increasing meat production, enhancing milk yield and quality, improving fiber characteristics, and developing specific breed traits. Breeding objectives often depend on market demand, consumer preferences, and the specific niche in which the enterprise operates.

- **Selection and genetics**: To achieve the desired breeding objectives, commercial breeders carefully select superior breeding stock with desirable traits such as growth rate, carcass quality, milk production, disease resistance, and temperament. They may employ selection methods such as performance testing, pedigree analysis, and genetic evaluations to identify animals with superior genetic potential.

- **Breeding systems**: Commercial goat breeding operations usually employ various breeding systems. Some common systems include the following:

  - **Purebred breeding**: This system involves breeding animals of the same breed to maintain the breed's purity and preserve its specific characteristics. Purebred breeding leads to breed improvement and quality standards.

- o **Crossbreeding**: Crossbreeding involves mating animals from different breeds to combine desirable traits from each breed. This approach aims to achieve hybrid vigor or heterosis, which improves performance, growth rates, and overall productivity. Crossbreeding can also develop new breeds.

- o **Grading up**: Grading up involves using a superior purebred buck to breed with grade goats (typically crossbred animals). The offspring are then bred back to purebred bucks, gradually improving the overall genetic makeup of the herd.

- **Reproduction management**: Effective reproduction management involves monitoring estrus cycles, implementing controlled breeding programs, and ensuring optimal mating practices. This crucial process can utilize artificial insemination (AI) and other techniques to introduce superior genetics and maximize breeding efficiency.

- **Health and disease management**: Commercial breeders prioritize animal health and implement robust disease prevention and management protocols. Vaccinations, regular health checks, and biosecurity measures ensure the herd's well-being. Timely treatment and prompt intervention of illness or disease outbreaks help maintain herd productivity.

- **Nutrition and feeding**: Adequate nutrition is vital for optimal animal reproduction, growth, and overall health. Commercial breeding operations focus on providing balanced diets that meet the specific nutritional requirements of each stage of the goat's life cycle. This may involve a combination of pasture grazing, supplemental feeding, and formulated rations tailored to meet the herd's nutritional needs.

Commercial goat breeding requires genetics, animal husbandry, and business management expertise. These operations are vital in meeting the increasing global demand for goat products while striving for genetic improvement and sustainable profitability.

Chapter 14: Health and Disease Management

Health and disease management is integral to raising goats commercially because it ensures the animals' overall well-being and the operation's success. Farmers can prevent diseases, minimize health risks, and maintain a productive and thriving goat herd by implementing effective health management practices.

Overview of Common Goat Diseases and Parasites

As a goat farmer, you must know about common diseases and parasites that may affect your herd. Promptly identifying and managing these conditions can help maintain the health and productivity of your goats.

Here is an overview of some common goat diseases and parasites:

Internal parasites (gastrointestinal worms)

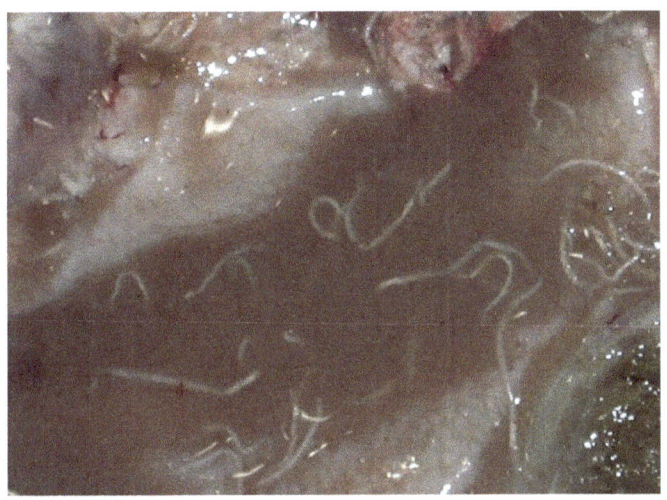

Goats are susceptible to various internal parasites, including roundworms (Haemonchus contortus), tapeworms, coccidia, and lungworms. These parasites can cause diarrhea, weight loss, anemia, poor growth, and even death if left untreated.

Regular fecal testing and strategic deworming protocols are the best way to control internal parasites.

External parasites

Flea   Louse   Tick

External parasites like lice, mites, fleas, and ticks can cause irritation, hair loss, skin lesions, and decreased production.

Effective parasite control measures, including proper hygiene, regular grooming, and approved topical treatments, are the best way to prevent infestations.

Caseous Lymphadenitis (CL)

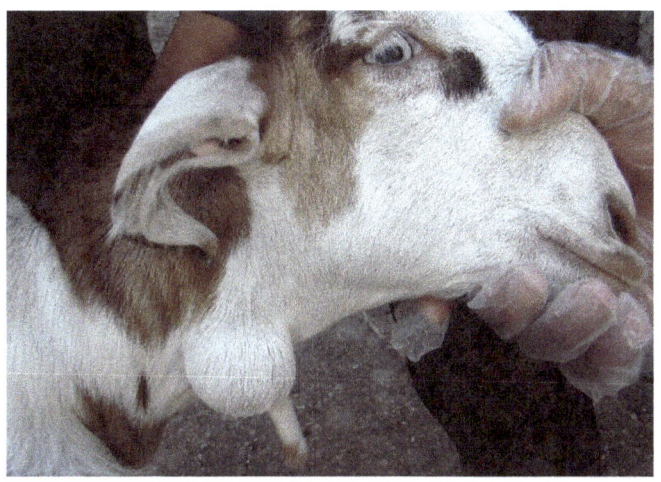

CL is a chronic bacterial infection caused by Corynebacterium pseudotuberculosis. It primarily affects the lymph nodes and can lead to abscess formation. CL is highly contagious and can spread through direct contact or contaminated environments.

Therefore, isolate infected animals, drain, and effectively dispose of the abscesses to prevent transmission.

Foot rot

Foot rot is a bacterial infection that affects goats' hooves, causing lameness, swelling, and pain. Fusobacterium necrophorum is the most common cause of this condition.

Proper trimming, regular hoof inspection, and maintaining clean, dry living conditions can help prevent and manage foot rot.

Caprine Arthritis Encephalitis (CAE)

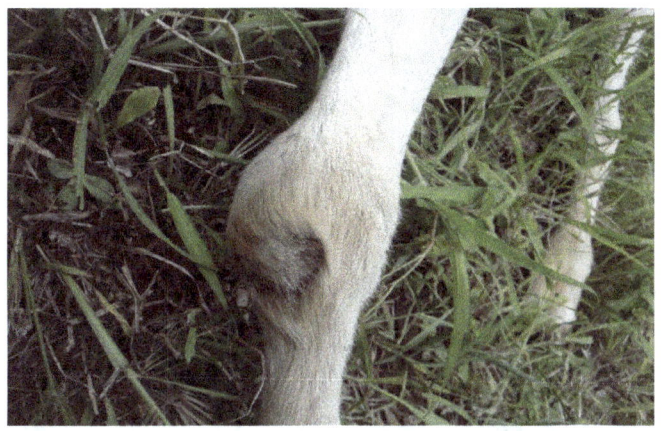

CAE is a viral disease that affects goats and can lead to arthritis, encephalitis (brain inflammation), and mastitis. Transmission happens through infected colostrum, milk, and respiratory secretions.

The main preventive measures are testing and removing infected animals, pasteurizing milk, and avoiding shared equipment between infected and uninfected goats.

Scrapie

Scrapie is a fatal, degenerative disease affecting goats' central nervous system. Prions cause it and can lead to weight loss, behavioral changes, and death. Scrapie usually transmits through contact with infected animals or their bodily fluids.

Strict biosecurity measures are the best prevention option.

Pneumonia

Various bacteria, viruses, or other respiratory pathogens can cause pneumonia in goats. It can result from poor ventilation, overcrowding, or exposure to extreme weather conditions. Symptoms include coughing, rapid breathing, fever, and decreased appetite.

Proper housing, ventilation, vaccination against respiratory diseases, and prompt treatment of affected animals are the most potent ways to prevent and manage pneumonia.

It is worth noting that this is not an exhaustive list of all possible goat diseases and parasites. Consult a veterinarian experienced in goat health to develop a comprehensive health management plan tailored to your specific farming practices, geographic location, and herds' needs.

Vaccination and Preventive Healthcare Measures

Vaccination and preventive healthcare measures are perhaps the best way to keep your goats healthy, especially in a commercial goat-raising enterprise.

Implementing a proactive approach to disease prevention can help minimize the risk of illness, reduce production losses, and ensure the longevity of the herd.

Let's explore the importance of vaccination and preventive healthcare measures in detail:

Vaccination Programs

Developing a comprehensive vaccination program helps protect goats against common infectious diseases. Consult a veterinarian to understand the appropriate vaccines based on the prevalent diseases in your region and the specific needs of your herd.

Vaccines are available for diseases such as clostridial infections, respiratory illnesses, and reproductive diseases. Follow the recommended vaccination schedule and ensure all goats receive booster shots for continued protection. Regularly review and update the vaccination program to address emerging diseases and changing herd health requirements.

Parasite Control

Implementing an effective parasite control program helps prevent the negative impact of internal and external parasites on goat health and productivity.

Regularly deworm goats using appropriate anthelmintic medications as per veterinary recommendations. Consider conducting fecal examinations to monitor parasite loads and identify any resistance to deworming medications.

Practice pasture management techniques, such as rotational grazing and proper manure disposal, to reduce the risk of parasite re-infestation. Maintaining hygiene in housing areas and regularly cleaning and sanitizing water and feed containers can also contribute to effective parasite control.

Biosecurity Measures

Biosecurity measures are another way to prevent the introduction and spread of infectious diseases within the herd.

Limit access to your premises by implementing controlled entry points, requiring visitors to follow biosecurity protocols, and quarantining newly acquired goats to monitor their health status before introducing them to the rest of the herd.

Avoid sharing equipment, such as feeders and water troughs, between different groups of goats to minimize disease transmission.

Regularly clean and disinfect equipment and facilities to reduce the risk of pathogen buildup.

Nutrition and Hygiene

Proper nutrition and hygiene practices can help your goats maintain good health and immune function.

Provide a well-balanced diet that meets their nutritional requirements and supports their immune system. Always ensure your goats have access to clean and fresh drinking water.

Maintain clean and well-ventilated housing facilities by regularly removing manure and providing appropriate bedding materials. Properly manage feed storage to prevent mold and spoilage.

Regular Health Checks

Perform routine health checks on goats to monitor their overall well-being and promptly address any signs of illness. Observe goats for changes in behavior, appetite, or appearance, and consult a veterinarian if you detect any abnormalities. Regularly trim hooves, provide dental care, and monitor body condition scores to maintain optimal health.

Working closely with a veterinarian and staying informed about the latest developments in goat healthcare will further enhance the effectiveness of preventive measures and contribute to the long-term success of the commercial goat-raising enterprise.

Chapter 15: Technology Advancements in Goat Farming

Technology advancements in goat farming are revolutionizing the industry and providing numerous benefits to commercial raisers. Integrating various technological tools and systems has significantly improved efficiency, productivity, and farm management.

Here is an in-depth look at the key technological advancements in goat farming:

- **Automated feeding and milking systems**: Automated feeding systems like robotic feeders allow for precise and efficient feed distribution to goats. These systems are programmable to provide individualized feed portions based on the nutritional requirements of each goat, reducing wastage and ensuring optimal nutrition. Similarly, automated milking systems enable efficient and hygienic milking processes, reducing labor requirements and improving milk quality and quantity.

- **Remote monitoring and data collection**: Remote monitoring systems utilize sensors and smart devices to monitor various aspects of goat health and farm conditions. These systems can track parameters such as body temperature, activity levels, rumen pH, and water consumption. Real-time data collection and analysis promotes early detection of health issues, timely intervention, and improved overall herd management. It provides valuable insights into herd performance, allowing farmers to make informed breeding, nutrition, and health management decisions.

- **Precision nutrition management**: Precision nutrition management involves using advanced technologies to measure and control the nutritional intake of goats. This includes automated feeding systems that dispense precise amounts of feed based on individual goat requirements and software programs that calculate and formulate balanced rations. Precision nutrition management optimizes growth, milk production, and overall health by accurately meeting each goat's nutritional needs.

- **Genetic selection tools**: Genetic selection tools, such as genotyping and genomic selection, transform how we breed goats and select them for desirable traits. These tools make identifying goats with superior genetic potential for traits like milk production, fiber quality, disease resistance, and conformation easier. By incorporating genomic information into breeding decisions, farmers can accelerate genetic progress, improve herd quality, and achieve their production goals more efficiently.

As a commercial goat farmer, you must stay informed about the latest advancements, seek advice from industry experts, and invest in appropriate infrastructure and training to fully harness the benefits of technology in goat farming. Continuously monitor, maintain, and update technological systems to ensure proper functioning.

By embracing these technological advancements, you can unlock the full potential of your commercial goat-raising operation and stay competitive in the dynamic agricultural landscape.

Conclusion

In conclusion, commercial goat raising is a land of opportunity. Whether meat, milk, fiber, or breeding stock, beginners can capitalize on market demands and create a thriving business.

By focusing on efficient production practices, breed selection, and marketing strategies, you can meet the increasing demand for goat meat, supply the market with nutritious goat milk and its value-added products, tap into the luxury fiber industry, and contribute to improving goat breeds through selective breeding.

With careful planning and dedication, you can establish a profitable and diverse goat-raising operation, catering to multiple product markets and significantly impacting the industry.

If you enjoyed reading this book or found it helpful, please show your support by leaving an honest review on Amazon. Every review makes a difference!

Thank you for supporting indie authors; you're awesome☺

www.ingramcontent.com/pod-product-compliance
Lightning Source LLC
Chambersburg PA
CBHW072206290526
45794CB00004B/1667